The
WORST-CASE SCENARIO
Survival Handbook:
Junior Edition

The
WORST-CASE SCENARIO
Survival Handbook:
Junior Edition

Jefferson Twp. Public Library
1031 Weldon Road
Oak Ridge, NJ 07438
973-208-6244
www.jeffersonlibrary.net

By David Borgenicht and Robin Epstein

Illustrated by Chuck Gonzales

A⁺
Smart Apple Media

A WORD OF WARNING: It's always important to keep safety in mind. If you're careless, even the tamest activities can result in injury. As such, all readers are urged to act with caution, ask for adult advice, obey all laws, and respect the rights of others when handling any Worst-Case Scenario.

Published by Smart Apple Media, an imprint of Black Rabbit Books
P.O. Box 3263, Mankato, Minnesota 56002
www.blackrabbitbooks.com

This library-bound edition is reprinted by arrangement with Chronicle Books, LLC, 680 Second Street, San Francisco, California 94107

First Published in the United States in 2007 by Chronicle Books LLC.

 A QUIRK PACKAGING BOOK.

Worst-Case Scenario and The Worst-Case Scenario Survival Handbook are trademarks of Quirk Productions, Inc.

iPod, Cheerios, and Jell-O are registered trademarks of Apple Computer, Inc., General Mills, Inc., and Kraft Food Holdings, Inc., respectively.

Book design by Lynne Yeamans.
Typeset in Adobe Garamond, Blockhead, and Imperfect.
Illustrations by Chuck Gonzales.

Library of Congress Cataloging-in-Publication Data
Borgenicht, David.
  The worst-case scenario survival handbook : junior edition / David Borgenicht and Robin Epstein.
      pages cm
  ISBN 978-1-59920-976-0
  1. Social skills in children--Juvenile literature. 2. Socialization--Juvenile literature. 3. Children--Humor--Juvenile literature. I. Epstein, Robin, 1972- II. Title.
  HQ783.B663 2015
  646.700835--dc23
                          2013037222

Printed in the United States at Corporate Graphics,
North Mankato, Minnesota, 2-2014, PO 1644
10 9 8 7 6 5 4 3 2 1

CONTENTS

CHAPTER 3
Survival Skills for Your Social Life

CHAPTER 4
Survival Skills for the Outdoors 95

Introduction

You'll often hear adults say they wish they could be kids again. They say things like, "Oooh, childhood—such a delicious and carefree time of life! No responsibilities, nothing to worry about...why, it's practically perfection on a plate!"

Puh-lease!

After you've stopped snorting with laughter, don't you want to reply, "Um, *hello*? Earth to Oldie McMoldy! Do you *really* not recall what it's like to climb a mountain of homework every night? Could you have *possibly* forgotten what it's like to deal with the most annoying, wedgie-giving brother *ever*? Do you *honestly* not remember how hard it is to convince others *it wasn't you—it was the dog* that just farted right next to you?"

Being a kid is no cakewalk down Easy Street with an ice-cream cone in your hand. But there's plenty of fun to be had every day—as long as you know how to steer clear of the dog poo in your path. That's where this book comes in: It offers step-by-step instructions, clever comebacks, and excellent excuses that will help you breeze through tough times, side-stepping the poo with a smile on your face.

If you find yourself in a sticky situation at home—say, your allowance is skimpier than a teeny-weeny bikini, or your little sib won't stay out of your stuff—we have excellent solutions to help you deal. Maybe you got a bad report card, or it's picture day at school and you didn't know it—we've got strategies to help you cope. We even tackle the great outdoors, offering foolproof fixes if you have to walk to school in the worst weather or deal with things that sting.

If you experiment with some of the techniques we recommend, we bet you'll not only find some great solutions to life's little mysteries, you'll also have a blast!

—*David Borgenicht and Robin Epstein*

CHAPTER 1

Survival Skills at Home

How to Make Your Room Shipshape

If dirty laundry, trash, and toys are scattered all over your floor, these steps will help get the "CleanYourRoomImmediately" monkeys off your back.

1 Divide and conquer.
Start by finding all items of clothing and putting them into one pile. Next, gather up all pieces of trash and put them in a second pile. In a third pile, collect all your toys and the remaining random stuff.

2 Scoop and dunk.
Scoop all the contents of pile number one into the nearest laundry hamper. Wheel a garbage can up to pile number two, and perfect your slam dunk as you toss all of your trash into it (making sure to recycle recyclables!). Finally, see pile number three just sitting there in the middle of your room? Give yourself ten minutes to put away as many things as you can.

3 If you have anything left . . .

Still looking at a pile of stuff? Well, you won't see it if you shove it under your bed, will you? So don't dilly-dally—put that pile where the sun don't shine.

4 Make the bed by using the "breadspread."

Making a bed that you're just going to mess up later that night feels like a time waster. So don't think of this as making your bed. Think of it as topping your bed sandwich with "breadspread." Find the exact middle of your bedspread or comforter and place it in the center

Place the middle of your bedspread in the center of your bed.

Smooth down the spread.

Bin There, Done That!

Don't like chucking your stuff? Stacking crates, like the kind you buy at a housewares store—or the milk crates used at supermarkets—can be your best friend if you're the pack-rat type. You can store anything and everything in these bins. And because they stack on top of one another, they look tidy, which means you'll be able to fool people into thinking *you're* tidy, too.

of your bed. Now smooth down the spread so that its corners line up with the corners of the bed and the extra material drapes off the sides of the bed. *Voilà!* The results look good enough to eat!

5 **Make like a dog and sniff out any remaining problems.**

Starting at your door, get down on all fours, Fido-style. Let your nose lead you around the room to sniff out any overlooked socks or bags of cheese puffs. Dispose of your discoveries as appropriate.

6 Next time, convince, beg, or bribe someone to help you with the cleanup.

The more hands pitching in, the faster the job gets done. Old people realize this: That's probably why they had your younger sibling(s) in the first place. So recruit away. You might need to offer little sibs some sort of reward in exchange for their help. If so, tell them that by cleaning with you they'll learn the famous "make like a dog" trick (see step 5). The youngest of younger sibs might just go for that one!

> **BE AWARE** • Cleaning your room is a task that will need to be done again and again, unless you can think of a more permanent solution. You could take a vow of poverty and donate your possessions to charity, but that would mean giving away your favorite stuff. Or, you could try to convince your family that your mess is actually an art installation. It's okay if they don't completely grasp it—you are an avant-garde artist, which means you are ahead of the times.

How to Survive a Nosy Sibling

It's a fact of life: Brothers and sisters are always getting into each other's business. So, here's how to keep yours out of yours.

 Lights out.

Before leaving your room, unscrew all the light bulbs and pull your shades down. Store the bulbs in a dresser drawer for safekeeping and stash a flashlight there, too. When your sibling comes in, it'll be too dark for her to see anything.

 Let her know two can play the snooping game.

If Sis sneaks into your room, sneak into hers and "borrow" her favorite toy. When she demands you give it back, make her sign the "Staying Out of My Stuff" contract on page 126.

HOW TO KEEP YOUR JOURNAL SECRET

 Use a decoy journal.

Create a fake journal to throw the snooper off track, and hide it in a place you know the snooper will look. The entries in your fake journal should be believable enough that the snooper stops looking for the real journal. Or, you could address the snooper directly, like this: "I get the feeling my little bro found my journal. He's probably reading it now, *aren't you, snoop*?! "

 Hide your journal in a super-hard-to-find spot.

Snoopers search predictable spots: under your mattress, at the bottom of your desk drawer, or in your book bag. So, hide your journal behind books on your bookshelf, fold it into a sweater you keep at the bottom of your dresser drawer, or tape it under the lid of a random shoebox.

Places to Hide Your Journal

Behind books on a shelf　　In a folded sweater　　Taped under a shoebox lid

How to Survive Being Grounded

Grounding takes many forms, but it always starts the same way: An adult has gotten steamed, and now he's determined to make you feel the heat. Try these ideas to make that "heat" a little less punishing!

1 Pretend you agree with the decision to punish you.

Adults believe that grounding teaches you a lesson. "Agreeing" with the grounding makes them think the lesson is being learned. Say, "I understand why you're grounding me. And if I were in your shoes, I'd ground me, too." Hold your laughter until you are safely back in your room.

2 Sleep it off.

If you're sent to your room, remember there's a very comfortable bed in there. Take this time to chill out and daydream.

3 Do that project you keep meaning to do.

Think of this period of "punishment" as an opportunity to kickstart your art project/science experiment/future as a guitar god.

4 Do the jailhouse workout.

Prisoners know that doing push-ups makes the time go by more quickly, with the added bonus of making their upper bodies strong. Just imagine the look on your personal jailer's face when you emerge from your holding cell with bulging biceps!

5 Renegotiate the terms of your punishment. Give the punisher some time to cool down, then calmly ask if she will consider letting you out early. Without cracking up, say, "I know what I did was wrong. I've learned my lesson. May I please be paroled?"

> **BE AWARE** • After you've spent a couple of hours doing arts and crafts in your room, you might discover something alarming: You don't want to leave! Don't get too freaked out. This is a common reaction to imprisonment, and the cure is simple. As soon as you get released from the slammer, call a friend and plan to hang out.

Arguments to Make If Your Stuff Gets Taken Away

 Television privileges: "If I can't watch TV, I won't be able to watch the Learning Channel. You want me to learn, don't you?"

 Video game privileges: "I don't play video games for fun—I play them to improve my hand-eye coordination. Don't foil my attempts at coordination, please!"

 Skateboard privileges: "But I need my skateboard to get to the flower shop in order to buy you a 'You're the Best Parent Ever' bouquet."

 Outdoor privileges: "Wouldn't it be better if I worked off my excess energy outside instead of in here, near your fragile valuables?"

 Mall privileges: "But I finally saved enough of my babysitting money to buy you that waffle maker you've been eyeing."

 Cell phone privileges: "But what if I get lost, or need to call to let you know I'm going to be a little bit late?"

How to Clean Your Plate of Something You Hate

"Enjoy!" your friend's mom says as she serves you something smelling like dirty socks. "Bon appétit!" cries the waiter, handing you a plateful of something that looks and smells like cat food. "Eat up!" instructs Grandma, giving you meatloaf she baked her dentures into. When you're a prisoner at the dinner table, there's no escaping till you deal with that meal.

 ## Sauce it up.

Disguise the taste of something disgusting with a generous helping of something tastier. To avoid getting caught, put the condiment on the *side* of your plate instead of pouring it directly on your food. Use your fork to push bite-sized pieces through the pool of sauce. Now lift that forkful of yuck to your mouth and stay focused on the taste of the sauce—chew quickly, swallow, and repeat.

Top 10 Flavor Savers

Here's a list of condiments and sauces that can really disguise a foul food.

1. Ketchup
2. Mustard
3. Salsa
4. Spaghetti sauce
5. Gravy
6. Barbecue sauce
7. Applesauce
8. Soy sauce
9. Tartar sauce
10. Relish

Sauce your food less obviously, of course!

 Breathe to relieve.

Once you start chewing, begin blowing air out of your nose in quick, short bursts. Concentrating on your breathing not only gets you to think less about the food, it prevents you from smelling it. The end result? You'll barely be able to taste it (because taste and smell are linked).

Flush it away.

If your meal is so bad that swallowing it is making you gag, then turn to your best ally in this situation: your drink. Chew a small portion of food at a time, and then take a sip of your drink to ease it down.

Bread it.

A simple dinner roll can be a lifesaver when you're faced with a dreadful dinner. Bread is especially good when you don't like the texture of your food (like if it's slimy). Just take a bite of bread with every bite of slime. The blandness of the bread will also help mask bad flavors.

Practice "Mind Over Meal."

In extreme cases, you may need to call upon your imagination. Consider it a challenge to see if you can imagine that the liver you're eating is actually a delicious grilled steak.

> **BE AWARE •** When food is spicy, drink milk instead of water to lessen the burn. Another heat-beater is buttered bread—the fat in the butter counteracts the heat.

Disguise it with mashed potatoes.

If you really can't deal with the taste, the thick white-ness of mashed potatoes provides the perfect cover for the horror on your plate. Lift the mashed potatoes with your fork, and slide that unwanted crud under the cloud of mashed mush using your knife. Other useful places to stow food are under a helping of peas or chunky applesauce. Try cutting your food into tiny pieces first—this makes it easier to hide.

How to Increase a Skimpy Allowance

You need more dough, simple as that. Here's how to get your parents to agree that you deserve a raise.

 Compare the going rate.

Find out how much allowance your friends get. Then write up a chart to show that you've done your research and your wages are lagging.

Money-Saving Tips to Make Do with What Ya Got

- **Create a budget and stick to it.**
  Decide you won't spend any more than *X* dollars a day.

- **Carry around very little cash.**
  If you don't have it on hand, you can't throw it away.

- **Keep a change jar and make daily deposits.**
  All those nickels and dimes add up.

- **Don't buy anything.**
  Sometimes the most obvious tip is the best of all.

 Acknowledge that with greater money comes greater responsibility.
Offer to spend more time with your annoying little sister if you get a pay bump.

 Be your own union.
Just like a labor union, negotiate for fixed raises once a year. Your birthday would be the perfect occasion.

Top 5 Ways to Get More Dough

1. Go couch diving.

Couch cushions are a magnet for change. Pull them up, and you're likely to locate some coins hiding deep in the couch cracks.

2. Do odd jobs.

Is it winter? Shovel snow for dough. Is it spring? Water the flowers for that green. Is it summer? Fan your family for some coin. Is it fall? Rake leaves for legal tender.

3. Rent out your toys.

If you're not playing with a certain toy anymore, rent it to another kid for a week and charge a set fee.

TOY RENTAL

4. Teach old folks how to use electronic equipment.

People used to say, "You can't trust anyone over thirty." Now people say, "You can't trust anyone over thirty to set up their own computer equipment." Offer your services to the nearest technically challenged oldster and teach her how to master her cell phone or laptop.

5. Become a short-order cook.

Offer to make special brown-bag creations for your classmates. They'll be glad to avoid the grub the cafeteria is serving.

How to Make Your Younger Sibling Bearable

Isn't it amazing how such little kids can be such big pains in the butt? Of course, *you* were young once, but you've grown out of it—so maybe there's hope for your smaller sibling, too. When you and Little You have to hang out together, there's no reason it can't be fun for the both of you ... especially if you figure out how to mold your sib into the perfect personal assistant.

Turn your sibling into a pack mule.

Tell your younger sib that if he's going to hang with you, he has to carry your backpack. And spare pieces of clothing in case you get cold. And your sweater if you get hot. If you want to be nice, tell him he doesn't *have* to carry your stuff on his head…but he'll get bonus points that way.

Make your sibling your personal messenger service.

In a time of e-mails and texts, it's unusual to get a hand-written note. Have a little sib hand-deliver your notes for you. It adds that extra-special personal touch that says, "I care enough to send my sister."

Insist that your sibling become your server.

Hungry? Thirsty? Just want a little snack? Sure, you could walk to the refrigerator to get that food or drink. Then again, why not have little bro do it for you? Tell him you're teaching him a skill he can use later in life when his career as a movie star doesn't work out.

BE AWARE • Make sure your sib knows that working for you is an honor. To prevent her from getting the idea that this will be a regular thing, have her sign a contract stating that she gets that this is a one-time-only deal (see the "Hang Time" contract on page 127). Also, make sure she understands that children in other countries would fight for the opportunity to spend time with you.

Top 10 Reasons You Shouldn't Be Saddled with Your Sib

1. Her nose runs even when she's sitting still.

2. He chews with his mouth open.

3. She's covered in crumbs!

4. He smells like milk.

5. She somehow manages to make things sticky just by looking at them.

6. He turns everything into a song, then sings it really loudly.

7. She keeps calling you by a nickname you don't want anyone to know.

8. He never qualifies for the "You need to be this tall to get in" rides.

9. Her Cheerios spill EVERYWHERE!

10. He can't even work a video game controller.

How to Soothe a Peeved Parental Unit

When an adult in your life is mad, your life gets harder (even if you weren't the one who got him or her ticked off). These ideas may make the dark clouds hanging over your parent's head pass faster.

1 Say the two all-purpose, virtually never-fail magic words: "I'm sorry."

Even if you're 100 percent sure you did nothing wrong, just say it. Then cock your head to the side, make your best puppy-dog eyes, and say it again as sincerely as possible: "I'm really, *really* sorry."

2 Avoid saying, "Wow, being angry at me really makes you look ridiculous."

Even though this might cross your mind, this sort of commentary is sure to refuel the flames of Mom's or Dad's anger. Refer to step 1 again for the only words you should be uttering right now.

Telltale Signs You've Got an Annoyed Adult on Your Hands

- Steam is pouring out of his nose or ears.

- Her arms are crossed and her foot is tapping, but there's no music playing in the background.

- She keeps pounding the kitchen table with her shoe.

- He's opening doors just so he can slam them shut.

- She's muttering to herself about living on a desert island with no distractions. No clutter. And no one else there to bother her!

- He's fluffing the pillows on the couch so loudly you can hear him three rooms away.

3 **Give that madman or crazy lady some room.**
Now that you've offered an apology, let Foul-Mood Morris or Mary have some space to be alone with his or her anger. Back away quietly and try not to do anything irritating.

4 **Offer comfort . . . comfort *food*, that is.**
Prepare the person's favorite snack and leave it in a place where you know he'll find it. Include a simple note containing a heart and your initials.

5 **Do something nice for Mr. or Ms. Angry Pants.**
Complete the chore you're always being bugged to do without being asked to do it. Your parents will not only be pleasantly surprised, they'll know it's a sign that you want to make things better.

BE AWARE • Sometimes being nice can backfire and lead to more punishment for no good reason. Continually gauge the mood of the parent in question, and back off if things seem to be heading south.

CHAPTER 2

Survival Skills at School

How to Ride the Bus without Getting Schooled

As if the fact that it delivers you to school weren't bad enough, the school bus can be a torture chamber on wheels. Spitballs fly, homework gets stolen, and wet willies are delivered at an alarming rate. But if you properly prepare yourself for the ride, you can turn your school bus into a mobile pleasure pad.

1 When boarding the bus, keep your head low but your eyes up.

This "modified turtle" positioning system alerts others that you're too cool to care what they're up to. You'll just walk to your seat, tough exterior shell in place, and no one will bother you.

2 Scope out the seat real estate.

Location is everything. First look for your friends, and if they're there, go sit with them. If you don't know anyone, an empty seat near the middle of the bus is your best bet. Steer clear of the far back, home to those who think they're hot stuff, and the far front, home to those who might consider the bus driver one of their best friends.

③ Turn on. Tune out.

Stick your ear buds in your ears, turn your music player on, and tune out the rest of the madness. Enjoy the relaxing sounds of your favorite tunes till the wheels of the bus stop rolling.

> **BE AWARE •** Some bus drivers assign seats on the first day of school, so it's important to choose your seat carefully that day.

Turtle

"Modified Turtle"
Positioning System

How to Get By When You're Late to Class

You don't know exactly how it happened, but you're late again! This is not good. If your teacher catches you, you're going to be in *big* trouble. That's why you're not going to get caught.

OPTION FOR THE BOLD: SNEAK IN

1 Lay the groundwork.

This option requires advance preparation. If there are any classes that you're likely to run late for, choose a friend who will be your accomplice. Then discuss the plan (see below) with your friend, and prepare a signal system you'll use when the need arises.

2 Get the attention of your friend inside.

If the classroom door is still open when you arrive, try to catch your friend's eye without calling attention to yourself. Make sure to avoid looking at the teacher or standing in the teacher's line of sight.

3 **Give your friend the "Tell me when" signal.**
This will let him know that it's time to watch for the right moment for your entrance. Good moments include when the teacher is writing on the board, when the teacher is talking privately with another student, or anytime the teacher is just not focused on the door. When the moment is right, your friend should give you the "Go" signal.

4 **As soon as you get the "Go" signal, go for it!**
Crouch low to the ground and make your way to your desk as quickly and quietly as you can. If your desk is far away from the door, see if there's a closer empty desk where you can make a pit stop. (And if you get caught, see more options on the next page!)

OPTION FOR THE SLIGHTLY LESS DARING: GIVE AN EXCUSE

⭐ **I'm a comedian in training!**

Say, "I'm not late…I was trying to make an entrance!"

⭐ **I'm just trying to be a model citizen.**

Tell the teacher, "I would have been here sooner, but I know we're not supposed to run in the halls."

⭐ **I'm a VIP!**

Offer your apologies—you had an early-morning audition that took *forever*.

⭐ **I forgot to reset my watch.**

Tell the teacher, "I'd be right on time if this school were in Kansas City!"

⭐ **I'm hurt!**

Enter crying, limping, and explaining that you just fell down the stairs.

> **BE AWARE** • Before you attempt to use the last excuse, make sure your school has stairs.

How to Survive Going "Splat" in the Cafeteria

The only thing worse than being forced to eat a school lunch is tripping while carrying it on your tray in the cafeteria. The good news: Now that your food's gone flying, you don't have to swallow it. The bad news: Everyone in school just saw you "eat it." Here's how to make that trip a little less bitter.

1 Pop up and dust off.

Stand up as soon as you can. The faster you can get up, the faster this nightmare is over. If you've spilled any food on yourself, or if you have skid marks down your pant legs, wipe yourself off to minimize the evidence that you were just airborne.

2 Scan the room for the reaction.

Determine if your fall was something only a few people noticed, or if it was seen and heard by every person in the cafeteria, including, but not limited to: other students, teachers, administrators, visitors, lunch ladies, and the janitor.

3 Laugh it off and take your bow.

Laugh at yourself. That way, if others join in, they're now laughing *with* you instead of *at* you. Then, if the whole cafeteria's watching, prove that you have a great sense of humor by taking a big bow. If only a small group of people saw the event, simply give them a salute and nod your head.

4 With your chin up, walk to your table and eat what remains on your tray.

To minimize embarrassment, do not dwell in your puddle of spilled milk. Walk away and sit down with your friends as soon as you can.

Top 5 Things to Yell After You've Hit the Ground

1. "Man down!"
2. "Food fight!"
3. "Duck and cover!"
4. "Thar she blows!"
5. "Stop, drop, and roll!"

How to Ace a Spelling Test without Spell-Check

Spelling isn't directly related to intelligence, but it is directly related to how we remember things. So here are some tricks that will help you recall words that you still feel like a nincompoop for mispelling—er, misspelling.

1 Come up with a clever memory aid.

These are known as mnemonic (pronounced "nih-MON-ick") devices. Say you have to write a thank-you note. Do you write it on stationery or stationary? Remember *E* is for "envelope," so it's *stationery*. Is it a school principle or principal? It's *principal* because he's your "pal." *Separate* or *seperate*? Remove "a rat" by "sep-a-rat-ing" it.

2 Sound it out, out loud.

By breaking the word into pieces, it becomes less scary.

③ Write the word in the air.

In a spelling-bee setting, you don't have the advantage of seeing how the word looks on the written page. Try writing the word in big letters in the air in front of you. This will help you visualize what you're trying to spell.

BE AWARE • Here is a list of commonly misspelled words. Don't let them fool you!

- apparent
- believe
- conscience
- discipline
- embarrass
- fiery
- guarantee
- hierarchy
- inoculate
- jewelry
- kernel
- license
- millennium
- necessary
- occurrence
- privilege
- questionnaire
- rhythm
- sergeant
- twelfth
- until
- vacuum
- weird
- xylophone
- yucca
- zoology

Source: www.yourdictionary.com

How to Survive a Trip to the Principal's Office

You may be guilty, you may be innocent, but there will be no trial: For you the principal is judge and jury. So when you get sent to his office, be lawyer-like and present your best case.

Neat hair

Clean shirt

Shined shoes

PRINC

1 **Dress like you're going to court.**

Since you probably can't change into a suit, make what you're wearing look more respectable: Tuck in your shirt, tie your shoes, smooth down your hair, and do your best to get that "you can't catch me" grin off your face.

2 **Silently listen to the charges against you.**

Don't butt in while the principal is talking. If you speak up while he's telling you what you've been accused of, you risk two things. One: giving away too much information. Two: ticking him off. So keep your trap shut.

Random Excuses to Offer the Principal When Nothing Else Is Working

- "I'm just trying to make my classmates look good."

- "I was sleepwalking."

- "Picasso didn't do his best work until he was in his seventies."

- "I'm so upset about the [insert major world current event] situation. It's affecting me terribly."

3 Address the principal with respect.

When it's your turn to talk, remember your manners and say your "please"s and "thank you"s, your "yes, ma'am"s and "no, sir"s. Since you're trying to convince the principal you're innocent, the more respectful you act, the less criminal you'll seem.

Maintain eye contact.

Don't blink.

Listen silently.

PRINCIPAL

4 **Maintain eye contact.**

Guilty parties tend to look down and away. By looking the principal directly in the eye, you'll appear more trustworthy. And don't blink too much—excessive blinking is a sign of lying.

5 **Don't be a rat.**

Don't blame someone else or use a classmate as a scapegoat. You want to get cleared of these charges, but not at the expense of another kid.

6 **When asked what happened, explain it quickly and clearly.**

Don't blah-blah-blah—the principal has heard a *million* excuses. Give him your side of the story, outlining details that present you in the best light.

7 **Wrap it up with "sincere" thanks.**

End your speech by thanking the principal for listening to your side and judging the situation fairly. (Adults love being appreciated for doing their job. Plus, saying "thank you" will make him feel guilty about inflicting harsh punishment.)

How to Survive a Bad Report Card

Grades happen. If your report card is covered in letters that cling to the lower end of the grading alphabet, here's how to reduce its impact when you hand it to an adult for their signature.

1 Be affectionate and complimentary but not obviously fake.

If your flattery before handing over the report card is too over-the-top, your signer will smell something's up. Find a medium-sized compliment (something big enough to put her in a good mood, but not so big that it's obviously a lie) and give it with a smile.

2 Ask your signer to sit down—there's something you need to discuss.

Make sure she takes a comfy chair—you sit in something wooden and uncomfortable—then say you have something you need to talk to her about.

Top 3 Medium-Sized Compliments

1. "I don't think I've ever told you this before, but I think you've got a great sense of style."

2. "You are so much cooler than [insert name of friend or neighbor]'s [mom/dad]."

3. "You look like you've lost weight."

3 **Begin listing a series of real-life unfortunate events.**

Remind your signer that awful things are going on in the world, such as war, famine, and puppy torture. Then say, "All things considered, what I'm about to show you is not so bad."

4 **Present the report card, look down, and admit that no one is more disappointed in you than you.**

Say this without laughing.

5 **If your signer clasps her chest and falls off her chair after seeing your grades, call 911.**

While you wait for the ambulance, assure her that the report card is not really all that important, and that what she needs to focus on now is recovering.

6 **Place the pen in her hand and have her sign at the X.**

Before she's carted away, move her hand to sign the report card. Promise your signer that you will do better next term, and try to mean it.

Successful Folks Who Bombed in School

- **Woody Allen,** an Academy Award–winning writer, producer, and director, flunked motion picture production and English at New York University.

- **Napoleon Bonaparte,** one of the greatest military figures of all time, finished near the bottom of his class at military school.

- **Albert Einstein,** one of the world's greatest scientists, did terribly in elementary school, and failed his first college entrance exam.

- **William Faulkner,** a Nobel Prize–winning author, didn't graduate from high school because he didn't have enough credits.

- **Robert Kennedy,** former attorney general of the United States, failed first grade.

How to Get a Decent Photo on Picture Day

Most embarrassments fade fast. But a bad school photo lasts forever. Don't get caught looking like a weirdo in the yearbook. You'll never—and we mean *never*—live it down.

1 Water can help a bad hair day.

Woke up with crazy bed head? Realized you got hat head on the way to school? If you have no gel, try a tiny amount of hand lotion. Or simply go to the bathroom and wash your hands in warm water. Instead of drying them with a paper towel, run them through your hair.

2 Camouflage that pimple.

Remember, the size of your photo in the yearbook will be small. So even a *massive* zit will only be a mini-dot in the picture. The key is in minimizing its redness. If you have cover-up, lightly dot it around the area and smooth it into your skin.

3 Avoid patterns, stripes, or logos in favor of simple shirts in solid colors.

Go for light or bright solids that will make you stand out against the backdrop. Too much activity around your neckline distracts from the real subject of the photo—you! And besides, this year's coolest band could be next year's disgrace.

4 Use your best "I have a secret" smile.

The look on your face is by far the most important part of a yearbook picture. If you look happy or amused, the picture will turn out great. Think about the last time you laughed really hard. Be in *that* moment as the photo is being snapped.

Smile Examples

The "Saber-Toothed Tiger" Grin (NOT Recommended)

The "Smiling Is Hard" Look (NOT Recommended)

The "I Have a Secret" Smile (Recommended)

How to Eat Lunch by Yourself...and Enjoy It

No one to sit with at lunch? As long as you're properly prepared with things to distract yourself, it's really no big whoop. Plus, when you've got something cool going on, you may find people wanting to sit with you to see what it is!

Read something fun.

This is "you" time, so use it to read something interesting—a book, magazine, instruction manual, whatever.

Play a game or do a puzzle.

Sudoku, solitaire, and crossword puzzles are all one-person activities, so it's better that there's no one there to distract you anyway.

Do origami.

If you can't make a swan, at least try folding a fan.

Create the best music playlist ever.

Then come up with other "best ever" lists, like "best movies ever," "best pets ever," "best books ever," and so on.

Start writing your memoirs.

Call it what you want—diary writing, journaling, or memoir writing—it's always cool to have a record of your thoughts and daily activities. You never know: Years from now what you're writing might be what someone reads during *his* lunch period!

Draw your own map of the world.

Invent names for new countries, like Mybuttissosorenya and Boredoutofmyheadistan.

Pretend you're a private eye.

Like Harriet the Spy, take notes on what other people in the lunchroom are doing to improve your powers of observation for future espionage jobs.

How to Give an Oral Report without Passing Out

People list public speaking as the scariest thing in the world—even scarier than being eaten by an alligator. But it's not *that* bad. At most, it causes a few minutes of discomfort (whereas getting eaten by an alligator could, theoretically, go on for *hours*). These tips will make those minutes fly by.

1 ## Rehearse your material.

Being nervous only means you care about what you're about to say, so practice your report until you're comfortable with it. Rehearse it in front of a mirror. Rehearse it in front of your computer screen. Rehearse it in front of a friend. Rehearse when you're in the shower, before you go to bed, and when you wake up. After all that rehearsing, doing the real thing will seem as routine as brushing your teeth.

2 Warm up and chill.

Focus on your breathing. Inhale for three seconds, then exhale for three seconds. If you can excuse yourself to the bathroom right before your turn to speak, do some stretching exercises to help you relax.

3 No disclaimers.

No disclaimers means: never apologize, and don't announce, "This is going to be terrible!" These things just plant the idea that your presentation will be terrible (which it won't). Likewise, don't tell people you're nervous, because if you've followed steps 1 and 2 they won't know you're nervous unless you tell them.

4 Picture yourself giving a speech that's the cat's pajamas.

Imagine yourself in front of the class, speaking slowly, clearly, and smartly. If you can see it, you can be it!

5 Remember, your audience wants you to do well.

Since no one wants to sit through a bad, boring speech, it follows that most people genuinely want you to succeed. And if you suspect that there are a few meanies who *aren't* rooting for you, remember that doing well is your best revenge. So just to spite them, ace this talk!

Harness the Power of Creative Visualization

- **Picture the whole class dressed up like bunny rabbits.** What could be scary about bunnies?

- **Pretend you are an important historical figure.** You are giving a speech so powerful it wins the election or ends the war. Important historical figures don't slump or say "umm," so thinking of them should help you deliver your speech with dignity.

- **See yourself taking a deep bow when you are finished.** Imagine how deeply relieved you will feel.

6 **Focus on the subject of your speech, not the fact that you're giving one.**

Concentrate on the topic you're talking about. Think about all the interesting aspects of the subject that you want to get across to your listeners. This will help you think less about the fact that you're delivering a speech.

7 **Focus on the horizon.**

Instead of looking at someone who might make a face at you, keep your eyes focused just above your audience's heads.

> **BE AWARE •** Remind yourself to breathe—it makes you pause and slow down so that people can understand what you're trying to say. And if you remember to breathe, you'll avoid hyperventilating.

CHAPTER 3

Survival Skills for Your Social Life

How to Get Beyond a Bully

Bullies have been around since the time of the caveman. As soon as the first caveman realized (1) he was hungry and (2) he was bigger than the caveman next to him who was innocently eating a sandwich, the bully was born. Today's bullies still resemble that primitive man. It's time for you to teach them to evolve.

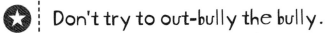

Don't try to out-bully the bully.

Being jerky back to the bully isn't smart (even if it seems so at the time). Bullies have bad reputations because they do bad things. Don't sink to their level.

Don't show fear or anger.

Bullies love nothing more than seeing their victims freak out. Your best reaction is to stay cool. You may be scared, but try to keep a straight face, a firm voice, and a nonshaky stance. This will show the bully you're just no fun to hassle.

Say "Stop," then walk away.

Simple but effective: Just tell the bully to knock it off. She knows that bullying is wrong, but since most kids won't tell her to stop, she'll keep doing it. When you say "Stop," it forces her to think about what she's doing.

Make a joke of it if you can.

It's hard to make fun of someone if she's doing a better job of making fun of herself. In fact, lots of professional comics got their starts trying to make bullies laugh. If people think you're funny, they'll be more interested in hearing your jokes than in hurting your feelings.

Make a Joke Out of It

When passing through bully territory, try to travel with a pal.

It's true: There is safety in numbers. Try not to be alone around the bully. Ever.

 Get help from someone even bigger—an adult.

If, after ignoring the bully, he just won't stop bothering you, let an adult know about it. A teacher, a parent, a guidance counselor—any of these people might be able to step in and make things better. Tell the person about the problem and then the two of you can figure out how to handle the situation without making it worse.

 Get support from your fans.

Let your true friends know what's going on, and talk about the bully situation with them. Then keep your friends in mind whenever the bully makes you feel down or stressed out. Remember that no matter what the bully says, you still have your cheering section. And *they're* the ones who really matter!

How to Make Friends When You're the New Kid on the Block

When you're new to town and know *no* one, life can seem like no fun. But think of this as a chance to start fresh. In a new town (or a new school), you can be whoever you want to be, including the most popular person around.

1 **Walk with confidence.**

You may be scared out of your mind on your first day at a new school, but try to be like an actor and act fearless. Keep your head up as you walk, make eye contact with other students, and then smile at them. If you can look cool and in control, people will believe you are. You might even convince yourself.

2 **When meeting people, lead with a compliment.**

People love getting compliments. Tell someone you meet that you like his shirt or hair. Then let the conversation unfold naturally.

3 Do the "Hello, my name is _____" routine.
Introduce yourself to the students sitting around you in
homeroom. Say hello to the person whose locker is next
to yours. Give a nod of the head and a smile to anyone
who looks in your direction. If she nods or smiles back,
find out what her name is.

4 Think of each day as a level in a video game. In any online role-playing game, you meet new people every day. You know advancing takes time, but you do so by learning the needs and wants of those around you. A new school is just like the start of a new game. Stay focused and play to win!

Fake It Till You Make It

Be prepared: It takes time to meet new people, and it takes even more time to meet new people that you actually click with. So until you have a group of friends you're proud to call your own, here are some ideas to help you deal with any awkward alone times.

- **Look casual.** Read a comic book, chill to your iPod, or customize your cell phone. You'll enjoy yourself and up your chances of attracting people with similar interests.

- **Try the old "I'm late for a very important appointment" routine.** If there's no one to hang with and you're getting bored or self-conscious, look up like you just forgot something, check your watch, and walk away quickly.

How to Survive Farting in Public

Call it what you will—a butt burp, a cheek flapper, a trouser trumpet, breaking wind, or cutting the cheese—sometimes you've just got to let one rip. Here are a few ways to keep people from thinking that you've got a lion roaring in your underpants.

The farter continues normal activity and provides no expression of guilt.

Block that fart!

Depending on where you are, grab a towel, jacket, or sweatshirt (anything made of thick, bulky fabric will do). Place it behind your behind and fart into it. The fabric will help mute the sound and absorb the smell. Now get as far away from that smelly towel as quickly as you can.

 ## Cough-a-fart!

If you feel as if you're about to let a fanny bubble fly, start coughing very loudly. Keep coughing until after you've finished making that "joyful noise."

 ## Put on your best "Who, me?" look.

Say you've launched a fart of the SBD (silent but deadly) variety, and it's not immediately obvious who brought the stink. Don't yell, "P-U! That smells!" because everyone knows that he who smelt it dealt it. Just quietly make a "wasn't me" face to disassociate yourself from the smell.

BE AWARE • If you're coughing, even though *you* can't hear the fart, others still might. So just to be on the safe side, if you're sitting down, try moving the chair to make its legs scrape the floor at the same time.

What to Say After You've Launched an Air Biscuit

If, despite your best efforts, your fart goes public, try saying one of these lines to turn it into a joke.

- "Well, there's no point in having a tush if you can't let it rejoice in song!"

- "Keep calling, sir! We'll find you!"

- "Hey, did somebody step on a duck?"

Fart Facts

- The average person farts about 14 times a day—whether she realizes it or not.

- Boys and girls fart with the same degree of frequency.

- Because cows graze on gas-inducing grass, they release so much methane gas every day that their farts contribute to global warming.

How to Outsmart a Prankster

The bottom line is this: If you want to learn how to stop pranksters in their tracks, you must first learn their tricks.

GIVING A WEDGIE

1 Prankster casually approaches his victim.
He can either sneak up on the victim from behind or cause a distraction. Example: He drops a pen, then asks the victim to pick it up.

2 The prankster grabs the victim's underpants and yanks them straight to the heavens.
The prankster digs for the top edge of the victim's briefs and pulls them as high as he can, just like he's pulling up a sock.

3 Prankster runs for the hills.

FOILING THE WEDGER

⭐ Wear low riders.

Fold the waistband of your underpants down until they ride low on your hips.

⭐ When the prankster has you by the waistband, yell, "Look out behind you!"

Because the prankster already has wedgies on the brain, he might assume he's about to get wedged himself. In his surprise, he may turn around and release you.

GIVING A WET WILLIE

1 Prankster licks her index fingers.

The prankster might pretend she's about to whistle with her fingers, sticking her index fingers in her mouth and licking them till they're good and wet.

2 Prankster approaches her victim, leans in, and squints at his or her nose.

By staring at another part of the victim's face, she'll take the "vic" by surprise.

3 As victim goes cross-eyed, trying to see what the prankster is looking at, prankster sticks her wet fingers into victim's ears.

The wet-willie giver will then twist those fingers around several times.

4 Prankster runs for the hills.

FOILING YOUNG WILLIAM

★ Know the usual suspects.

Pranksters are a special breed, especially the kind that have wet willies in their repertoire. (Who wants someone else's earwax on their fingers?) So keep a mental list of these potential prank perpetrators, and when one of them starts squinting at your nose, step away "willie" fast!

★ Pants the prankster mid-willie.

If you *do* get "willied," try to retaliate. Since the prankster's hands will be busy in your ears, he'll be defenseless. Take this time to yank his pants down.

Things You Can Do to Stop Yourself from Screaming

Prank pulling is only fun when it gets a great reaction—like a blood-curdling scream. So if you can practice *not* shrieking like a banshee, chances are, your days as a prank victim are running out. Here's how to avoid giving the prankster the satisfaction.

- Bite down on your lip.

- Cover your mouth with both hands.

- Close your eyes tightly and think of a walrus.

- Turn the scream into the first notes of the national anthem.

How to Make a Quick Fix on a Fashion Disaster

Your pants split. Your zipper broke. You've got a *giant* gob of gum in your hair. Whatever your problem, it doesn't have to be a disaster.

SPLIT PANTS

You just bent down to tie your shoe, and you heard *RRRRIP*! Here's what to do to keep your undies out of view.

 **Mask it.**

If you can locate masking tape (or duct tape), tape over the split. Then, use the next technique to cover the tape (since tape isn't much of a fashion statement!).

⭐ **Wrap it.**

Take your coat, sweater, or an extra shirt and wrap it around your waist, knotting the sleeves in front.

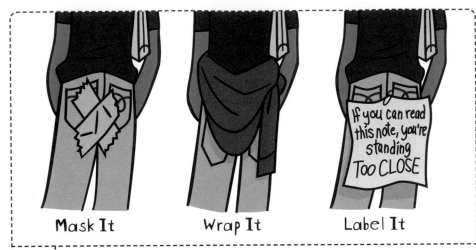

| Mask It | Wrap It | Label It |

Label it.

If all else fails, tape a sign to your butt that says, "If you can read this note, you're standing too close."

GUM IN YOUR HAIR

You've just blown your biggest-ever bubble. But as it bursts, your greatest achievement turns into a gummy nightmare. Tons of gum is now stuck in your hair. But don't reach for the scissors yet—try these ideas first.

Dab the gummed-up hair with cotton balls soaked in rubbing alcohol.

Rubbing alcohol reduces the stickiness of the gum and helps it slide off your hair.

Rub in some peanut butter.

Leave the peanut butter on the gummed-up hair for a few minutes. Now you should be able to rub the gum out. Wash your hair as soon as possible to remove the peanut butter smell!

 Apply baby oil or olive oil.

The gum should slide right off.

BROKEN ZIPPER

Sometimes the problem with a zipper is that it keeps sliding down. Other times the stupid thing just won't go up. Both problems can be solved with a safety pin. (For this reason, it's always a good idea to keep a safety pin or two stowed in a pocket of your book bag. If you don't have one, though, ask a teacher if he or she has an extra one lying around.)

 Don't call attention to the problem!

Instead, calmly slide a textbook (or binder or backpack) over your fly to cover the area. Then, as coolly as possible, excuse yourself to the bathroom, where you can deal with the problem in private.

For the sliding zipper, create a no-slip handle.
Hook the safety pin through the square opening at the bottom of the zipper pull. Now tug the zipper as high up as it will go and pierce it through the fabric on the top side of your fly. Pinch the pin closed.

 For the no-budge zipper, create a "butterfly" closure.
Pierce the safety pin through the middle of the outer edge of your fly. Now pierce the pin through the fabric on the outside edge of your zipper and close the pin. Yes, you'll have a safety pin through the middle of your fly, but this will allow you to keep your privates private till you can change pants.

"Butterfly" Closure   No-Slip Handle

How to Take the Bite out of Braces

Sure, you know there's a pearly white light at the end of the tunnel. The straight teeth you're going to have when your braces come off will look incredible! But right now you've got a mouthful of metal—or "clear" plastic—and it ain't pretty (especially not after a meal). Still, there's no need to be ashamed of that tin grin. If you follow these steps, you can flash your grill with pride.

 ### Brusha, brusha, brusha.

Braces tend to be food magnets, and you can often find a second meal from what gets trapped in your brackets alone. Pretty gross. Plus, trapped food makes your breath stink. The key is brushing your braces after every meal. But brushing isn't nearly as annoying as you might imagine, especially if you try to think of it as a chance to enjoy a minty-fresh dessert. (This will require some imagination on your part.)

Choose foods that soothe.

There's no way to sugarcoat the fact that your teeth will hurt when you first get braces. But that doesn't mean you have to limit yourself to things you can suck up with a straw. Treats like ice cream, pudding, and Jell-O are great for sore mouths. And guess what? They taste great, too!

 ## Don't drool, fool!

Yep, it's true that you drool more when you have braces. This is because the braces trick your mouth into thinking you've got food in there. And since you're not going to put a sponge in your mouth to stop the saliva flow, keep a handkerchief handy to wipe off your chin every now and then.

> **BE AWARE** • Attempts to hide your braces (covering your face with your hair or never smiling) will only backfire. People will start to wonder why you're always moping. Braces are only temporary, so while you have them, wear them with pride.

Top 5 Foods to Avoid Till You're Braces Free

Once upon a time, before you got your braces, these foods were fun to eat. Now they're just a sticky glue that's sure to get stuck in your wires.

1. Corn on the cob
2. Popcorn balls
3. Gum
4. Taffy
5. Caramel apples

If you know you'll be unable to resist gooey treats, carry an "interproximal brush" with you. This cone-shaped brush is designed to access tricky spots. Clean your braces right after eating, before food can harden.

How to Shake, Rattle, and Roll through a School Dance

Last place you wanted to be was at a school dance. But for whatever reason, here you are, in the school gymnasium, feeling unsure of what to do next. Since you definitely don't want your art teacher to ask you for a pity dance, you need to act fast.

IF YOU WANT TO DANCE...

 ### Ease into the groove.

If you're not all that comfortable on the dance floor, take it slow at first. You don't have to move a lot to be "dancing." Simple is good—maybe just a side-to-side sway with a little bounce to the beat. Use this time to scope out the dance floor. If you see a decent dancer, study that person's moves and see which ones you can...ahem...steal.

BE AWARE • While dancing, it's important to avoid the bad habit known as "the overbite," when you bite your lower lip with your front teeth. Keep your mouth relaxed and *smile* instead.

Smile, baby!

Your smile is by far your best dance move. It makes people *want* to dance with you, and it spreads the good times around (smiles are extremely contagious). And if you start to worry about what people think of your dance maneuvers, smile *more*. It'll make people think you're having more fun than they are, and soon enough they'll probably be trying to . . . ahem . . . steal *your* moves!

IF YOU DON'T WANT TO DANCE...

⭐ ### Help out.

You can't dance if you're manning the refreshment stand. So get behind that table and start ladling the punch. Or see if you can help the deejay spin.

⭐ ### Pull out your cell phone.

Talking on the phone is a perfectly good excuse for not being out on the dance floor. If you have someone to call, that's a bonus, but if not, you can simply pretend. If someone comes over and wants you to dance, give him the "just a minute, please" index finger, followed by a point to your phone and then the "chatty mouth" hand gesture. He'll quickly get the idea and leave you alone.

Start a card game.

No one says you have to be dancing to be the center of activity. So bring a few decks of cards and a bag of pretzels, and recruit a few other players for a game. As soon as other kids see what you're up to, they'll want to join in, too.

Smooth Ways to Ask Someone to Dance

Flying solo and dancing with a group of friends are both acceptable options, but if you want to ask someone to dance with you, here are some easy ways to ask.

- "I bet you and I would be the best dancers out there if we gave it a shot."

- "Do you know how to dance?" If the person says "Yes," reply, "I dare you to show me." If the person says "No," respond, "I can teach you!"

- "Would you like to dance?" If the person says "No," say, "I didn't think so. I just didn't want to be rude before asking your friend."

How to Survive an Embarrassing Adult

It's an age-old question: Are embarrassing adults born or made? Hard to say. And they're even harder to handle. There are two basic ways of dealing with embarrassing adults: a tough "right back atcha" method or the gentler "moral high ground" approach.

THE "RIGHT BACK ATCHA" METHOD

 Embarrass them back.

Start speaking in pirate talk by adding "Aaarggh!" and "To the plank with you, matey!" to the end of your sentences. Alternatively, you could pretend you are an alien. Comment on how welcoming the people of this planet have been and say, "You must visit me on Mars sometime. Bring the kids." Soon enough, whatever uncomfortable behavior the adult is doing will stop as she tries to figure out how to make *you* stop embarrassing *her*.

 Become the interrupting cow.

There's an old joke that goes like this:

Me: *Knock, knock.*

You: *Who's there?*

Me: *The interrupting cow.*

You: *The interrupting cow wh—*

Me: *Moooo!*

When your adult starts saying something terrifically embarrassing, interrupt the conversation by mooing at him.

THE "MORAL HIGH GROUND" APPROACH

 ## Justice is blind and so shall you be.

If said adult does something incredibly awkward (like picks a wedgie or nose, his or someone else's), pretend you have temporarily gone blind and didn't see it. Making the "How could you do that? I'm *so* embarrassed" face will only make the situation worse.

 ## Ask for a private moment.

Pull the offending adult aside, out of earshot of everyone else. In a calm voice, explain that you feel uncomfortable, and would she please stop doing X? Stress that you know she's not trying to embarrass you, but you're just feeling extra-sensitive today.

 ## Make an advance plan.

If you'll be with someone who is likely to bring up the most embarrassing thing about you—say, the fact that you used to shove crayons up your nose because you liked the way they smelled—make an agreement that certain topics will not be raised and that comments like "She still misspells her name" will be avoided.

CHAPTER 4

Survival Skills
for the Outdoors

How to Walk to School in Nasty Weather

How many times have you heard the old refrain "When I was a kid I had to walk to school in three feet of snow—uphill"? And how many times have you wanted to reply, "Yeah, but that was back in the Ice Age!" If you find you have to head out into the storm yourself, here's how to weather it gracefully.

Gear Up

1 **Gear up.**

Before stepping outside, kit yourself out in foul-weather gear: ski goggles, expedition-weight parka, hooded raincoat—whatever the weather dictates. Serious gear will prevent you from turning up in class looking like a drowned rat.

2 **Make your footwear watertight.**

Should your boots be nowhere in sight (or too hideous to wear!), you can prevent your feet from facing water torture. Just follow these steps:

- *Find two small plastic bags that will fit over your shoes.*
- *Put one foot in the center of a bag and pull the bag up around your leg.*
- *Wrap masking tape tightly around the bag just under your knee.*
- *Repeat with other foot.*

BE AWARE • Though plastic-bag booties may look stylish, they're not terribly sturdy. To prevent them from tearing—and yourself from skidding—avoid running while you're wearing them.

3 Use your umbrella as a shield.

Umbrellas aren't just for raindrops falling on your head. When rain and snow are being blown into your face, aim your umbrella slightly forward like a shield, to block the onslaught. Just make sure to peek out from behind the umbrella every so often to see where you're going.

Clever Excuses to Stay Home in Bad Weather

- "You don't want me to melt, do you?"

- "I'm already having a bad hair day. This is just going to push me over the edge, and you don't want to be responsible for that."

- "Since I don't have windshield wipers on my glasses, I won't be able to see where I'm going."

- "All the acid rain could burn holes in the new clothes you bought me."

- "This weather is literally a sign from above that I should stay home today."

How to Survive Outdoor Chores

It's a sunny day. You *should* be playing outside. But someone else—someone clearly too old to remember the definition of the word *fun*—has other plans for you.

RAKING LEAVES

Though they were pretty when they were on the trees, now that they're scattered all over the lawn they're suddenly a problem—*your* problem. But some skillful rake action can clear that right up.

1 ## Get it straight.

Veteran rake handlers have a secret: They rake in straight lines from the "bottom" of the lawn to the "top" (or vice versa) so it's always clear what section of the yard they've just finished. Random raking can lead to confusion, and chances are you'll wind up doing certain sections twice, which will make your raking time last even longer.

❷ Pile it up.

Instead of making one giant pile, rake your leaves into medium-sized to small piles. If the wind is blowing, a big pile runs the risk of being blown all over the lawn. A big pile also increases the likelihood that some jokester will go cannonballing into your hard work.

❸ Bag it, man.

Get a large plastic garbage bag and lay it on the ground right near your first pile. Stick your feet in the bag's opening and slide them apart to open the bag wide. Now, with one hand, pick up the top edge of the bag, forming a triangle. With your free hand, start scooping those leaves into that bag.

Rake in straight lines from the "bottom" of the lawn to the "top."

SHOVELING SNOW

Snow days are awesome—until a shovel is put in your hand and you've got to clean up a mess you didn't even make. But think of it this way: Once you've finished shoveling, you can start pelting those who made you do the job with some really primo snowballs.

① Don't put off till later what you can scoop faster now.

Snow that has just fallen is actually lighter and easier to shovel than snow that's been on the ground for a while. The longer snow stays on the ground, the more likely it is to partially melt and form a solid, heavy mass that's tightly packed and difficult to move.

② Don the uniform.

Make sure you've got good gloves, waterproof boots, a warm coat, a fuzzy hat, and a big ol' scarf wrapped around your neck before you start (corncob pipe optional). It's important to stay warm while you're shoveling, so bundle up. (You move more slowly when you're cold, so staying warm will help you get the shoveling over more quickly.)

3 Push the mush.

Instead of lifting the snow with your shovel, push it forward. Space your hands out on the shovel's handle—one toward the top, one closer to the bottom—because this increases your leverage. Better leverage makes the job easier. For the same reason, keep the shovel close to your body, too.

> **BE AWARE** • Once you've pushed the snow off the area you're trying to clean, don't throw it over your shoulder. The twisting movement can strain your back muscles.

Push the Mush | Don't Do the Twist

WASHING THE FAMILY CAR

Is there anything sadder than a car window begging, "Wash me"? If a note like this has been etched in the dust of your family's car, grab a bucket, a sponge, and some soap, because it's time to make that ride of yours shine.

1 ## Make bubbles.

Put your soap in a large (clean) plastic bucket, then fill the bucket with cool or warm water. You might be tempted to use hot water, but that's not good for the finish, so "stay cool" in terms of water temperature.

2 ## Hose her down.

Remove excess dirt on the surface of the car before you start the real washing process. Spray the car with a hose, starting from the roof and working your way down to wet its whole surface. You don't need to use a lot of water, just enough to get 'er damp. (Note: When spraying, don't use high pressure, because this can scratch the finish.)

3 ## Suds it up.

Dunk your sponge or wash mitt into the soapy water and swirl it around to distribute the soap in the mixture.

Once your washing device is good and soaped, start cleaning the car from top to bottom, roof to wheels. Hose her down again to remove any traces of soap.

④ Pat that baby dry.

It's a good idea to dry off the car after washing it: If it's driven when wet, dirt particles from the road will stick, and you might have to do the whole job again! Get a few old cotton towels and gently blot the car's surface. Start at the top of the car and be gentle: You don't want to risk hurting the finish of the car you just spent so long trying to make look good!

How to Survive a Canine Encounter

They say dog is man's best friend. But even a best friend can get snappy sometimes, and this one has a sharp set of teeth. Here's how to handle a pooch like a pro.

DON'T TOUCH A HAIR ON HIS HEAD

Be smart about introducing yourself to a dog you don't know.

★ Ask the owner before petting a pup.

Since all dogs have different personalities, it's important to ask the owner if the dog is friendly. You never know: That innocent-looking pup could have a ferocious bite.

★ Say yes to sniffing.

One of the ways a dog gets to know people is by sniffing them. So if your new four-legged friend starts nosing up to you, don't be scared, just hold the back of your hand out to him so he can catch your scent.

Say Yes to Sniffing

 ## Pet under the chin or on the chest.

Once you've gotten permission from the dog's owner, you should first stroke the dog on her chin or chest so she can keep an eye on your hands. If you pat the top of her head, she might think you're about to hit her!

 ## Step away from the bone.

Leave her alone when she's eating or chewing on a bone. She might think you're trying to take away her supper.

FOUR LEGS BEAT TWO EVERY TIME

If you're scared a dog might start chasing you and the owner isn't in sight, keep it cool.

① Don't start a race you can't win.

If you start running, you will only excite the dog's chase instinct. Don't jump up and down, either.

② Chill out.

Dogs are very sensitive creatures. If you freak out, that will probably cause the animal to do the same thing. If you want the dog to be peaceful, establish a peaceful mindset yourself. Hum your favorite song, dream about your favorite flavor of ice cream—whatever helps you get into a mellow mood.

③ Avoid eye contact and walk away slowly.

Once you've established the peace, you can slip away from the dog slowly and quietly (no sudden jerky movements). Looking into a dog's eyes is considered (by dogs, at least) to be an act of aggression. Avoid the temptation, or the dog may misunderstand you and think you want to fight rather than flee.

How to Deal with Poo on Your Shoe

You really stepped in it this time…and boy, does it stink! So many people hate getting poo on their shoes that many cities have passed "Pooper Scooper" laws, forcing owners to clean up after their pooches. But those laws don't help once you've gone skidding through a patch of poo. Here's how to make this humiliating situation a little less stinky.

PLEASE CLEAN UP AFTER YOUR DOG

1 **Do the "scrape, scrape, twist."**

To get the top layer of poo off your shoe, find the nearest curb and scrape your shoe—from heel to toe—against it. Repeat. Step in a shallow puddle if you can find one. Now locate a clean patch of sidewalk or grass and twist your foot around in it to loosen the deeper levels of doo in your shoe.

2 **Use a sole shovel.**

Take the sharp end of the stick or the blunt point of a pencil and begin digging it through the grooves in your sole. Pause to wipe it on the ground or on a piece of paper that you'll throw out later.

3 **Give your shoe a once-over with a damp paper towel.**

4 **Check for skid marks.**

Drag the shoe across a dry paper towel as a test. If the paper towel is skid-mark free, your work is done. If your shoe leaves a trail, repeat step 3 and test again.

5 **Wash your hands post-poo removal!**

How to Deal with Things That Sting

Okay, so your neighborhood isn't exactly the Amazon rain forest. But that doesn't mean there aren't plenty of dangerous creatures lurking around out there. These tips aren't 100 percent insect proof, but they'll keep you as stinger free as possible. You can use them to deal with bees, mosquitoes, wasps, horseflies, and any other pesky stinging insects.

 **Skip the perfume when you're outdoors.**
Insects are attracted to strong odors. If you know you'll be spending a lot of time outside, avoid using perfume, cologne, or even really smelly soaps.

Avoid tiptoeing through the clover barefoot.
How much would it stink—and hurt!—to get stung between your toes? A lot. But a bee can't tickle your tootsies if you're wearing shoes. So for feet's sake, put on your footgear.

Avoid dusk and dawn.

Mosquitoes are most active at these times of day. And avoiding dawn is yet another good excuse to sleep in!

 Don't wear brightly colored clothing.

Many insects respond to bright, wild colors and patterns (they think you're a flower), so put that vivid yellow shirt away for the day.

The SWAT Team

The best way to swat a fly or a mosquito is to use two hands. Although those little buggers might see one hand coming at them, their brains are too tiny to figure out what to do once a second hand appears. When you see a fly, slowly move your hands around both sides of its body. It will be so bewildered that you should be able to swat it simply by clapping your hands.

How Not to Avoid Bees

 Stay calm. Repeat: Stay calm.

If a bee lands on you, it will almost always leave on its own. It's just like a dog that wants to sniff you. If you start flapping your arms or shrieking, you risk making it defensive, which is when it's most likely to sting. If you can't wait for the bee to leave on its own, gently and slowly brush it away with a piece of paper.

IF STUNG...

Try to put mind over matter and convince yourself that you're not *really* crazy itchy. But if that doesn't work, give these suggestions a whirl.

> **BE AWARE** • If you start hyperventilating or having a hard time breathing, or if the stung area starts swelling like crazy, find an adult—or have a friend find one—*immediately*. You could be having a dangerous allergic reaction.

Ice it.

Numb the bite with an ice pack or ice wrapped in a towel.

Paste it.

Combine baking soda and just enough water to make a sticky paste and dab it onto your bite. Or, you can squeeze a little toothpaste onto the itchy area. Both pastes help dry out and shrink the bite.

Soap it.

Sometimes rubbing the itch with a bar of soap helps soothe the spot.

Whatever you do, don't scratch it.
You'll wind up making the itch worse, not better. If you must scratch, use your knuckles, since germs under your nails could cause an infection.

Unsavory Plants to Avoid

Insects aren't the only stingers in the wilderness. If you encounter either of these ghastly green growths, steer clear!

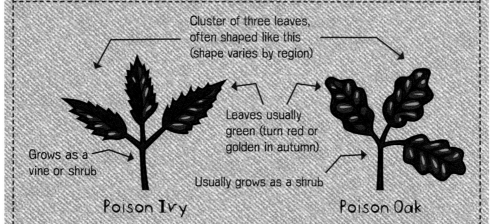

Cluster of three leaves, often shaped like this (shape varies by region)

Leaves usually green (turn red or golden in autumn)

Grows as a vine or shrub

Usually grows as a shrub

Poison Ivy

Poison Oak

If you *do* happen to touch one of these plants, act fast! Get an adult's help to clean your skin with rubbing alcohol or special soap designed to remove the itch-causing plant oils. Use plenty and rinse with lots of cool water—this is no time for moderation!

How to Handle a
Bicycle Misadventure

Wearing a helmet, using reflectors, and riding with care are the best ways to stay safe on your bike. But if you and your ride hit a rough patch, here's what to do.

SLIPPED CHAIN

You shift gears and suddenly the pedals lock up or you have zero resistance. What's up? Your chain has jumped the rails.

1 Turn your bike upside down.
To stabilize your bike, turn it upside down so it's standing on its seat and handlebars.

2 Catch the teeth.
Using your fingers or a stick, lift the chain and place it onto the teeth in the rear chain ring, and then onto the teeth in the front chain ring. The chain won't fit all the way around—it'll just hang loosely from the front ring.

Lift the chain and place it onto the teeth.

Catch the Teeth

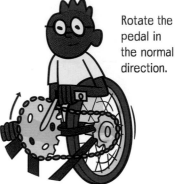

Rotate the pedal in the normal direction.

Rotate and Roll

3 **Rotate and roll.**

Keeping your fingers out of reach of the chain, grab the nearest pedal and rotate it very slowly in the normal pedaling direction. The chain should thread its way back on.

When You Need a Bike Doctor

Things went seriously wrong, and you (and your bike) went down. After you've picked yourself up and brushed off the dirt (you *were* wearing your helmet, right?), assess your bike. If you have any of the following issues, it's best to leave repairs to the pros:

- Bent frame or front fork
- Flat tire
- Broken chain
- Snapped brake cable

SLIPPERY ROADS

Slick roads are a bicyclist's nightmare. The best solution is to avoid riding in the rain at all. But if your sunny day ends in puddles and spray, here's what to do.

1 ### Survey the territory.

It takes a lot longer to stop when it's wet. Plus, roads are more slippery after a little rain, because the water mixes with surface oils. Be on the lookout for super-slick manhole covers, oily patches (look for rainbows), and fallen leaves.

2 ### Give it a brake.

Wet brakes take much longer to stop a bike, so test your brakes before you need to use them. Take it slow, and don't wait until you're flying out of control to start braking.

> **BE AWARE** • On wet roads, back-pedal gently or apply light pressure to your brakes—braking suddenly could cause you to skid.

3 **Keep your turns wide.**

A tight turn (or a swerve) on a slippery road ups your chances of spinning out. If you start to skid, reduce pressure on the brakes a little.

4 **Lighten up.**

Falling rain or spray from cars can make visibility poor for drivers. In these conditions, it's really important to wear bright clothing and have reflectors on your bike.

5 **Walk it off.**

If you're facing a steep downhill or pouring rain, remember that there's no shame in walking your bike!

Beware:
Slick roads=slick brakes

How to Survive Getting Lost in the Woods

Your family thought it would be a great idea to "get back to nature" and take a hike in the woods. Unfortunately, some of them have such a bad sense of direction they'd have trouble finding their way out of a paper bag! If those in charge have led you astray (a.k.a. gotten you lost), stay calm and suggest the following ideas.

1 Stop and re-step.
Once you realize you've wandered off the trail, go no farther. Retrace your footsteps to get back to the trail. Do *not* be tempted to take a shortcut—this can get you even more lost. Look for blazes (splotches of paint on trees) or cairns (rock piles)—these signs indicate the direction of the trail.

2 Don't panic.
Even if you're afraid you're really, really lost, a cool head will help you find your way home faster than a frantic one.

Prepare, Prepare, Prepare

The best way to avoid getting lost in the first place is to do some careful planning before you head into the woods. Make sure the adults you're hiking with have told someone at home where you are heading and are equipped with the following essentials.

- Map, plus guidebook or trail description

- Extra clothing: extra warm layers and a waterproof layer

- Extra water: at least 2–3 quarts (2–3 L) per person per day

- Water filter or treatment pellets

- Reliable fire starter (like waterproof matches)

- Food for the day (plus extra for an emergency)

- Whistle

- Sunscreen

- Insect repellent

- First-aid kit

This may sound like a lot of gear for a short day hike, and you will probably never need some of it. But if you *do* need it, you'll be very glad you have it!

③ Stick together.

You may be mad that your folks got you lost, but you don't want to make the situation worse by losing them, too. Stick close to your fellow hikers. The more of you there are, the better chance you'll have of attracting help.

Make sure you are equipped with essentials, including but not limited to: a map, extra layers (warm and waterproof), and extra water.

Thar she blows!

Make signals to help people locate you. Give your whistle three long toots, then wait and toot three times again in another direction. (If you forgot your whistle, just shout, "Help!") If someone calls back to you, wait for *them* to come to *you* and lead you back to the trail.

5 Hug a tree.

If help *doesn't* come right away, it's important to stay put. Wandering around off the trail could get you even more lost, or worse, injured. Find a warm, safe, visible spot and stay there.

6 Bundle up and take care of yourselves.

The key things you need to survive are water, warmth, and food. It's a lot harder to warm yourself once you've gotten cold, so put on your extra layers to retain your body heat. You wisely prepared your backpacks with emergency supplies before you left home (*didn't you?*), so now's the time to use them. Drink to stay hydrated, and eat your trail mix to stay nourished. And since you told people where you were headed and when you'd be back (*right?*), help should eventually come.

7 Graciously accept thanks.

Your companions will be *very* glad you made sure they were prepared. No need to say, "I told you so" (at least until you get safely home).

Appendix

USEFUL SCHOOLYARD COMEBACKS

The best tool to carry into the schoolyard is a sharp mind. The best comebacks make a person scratch his head as he tries to think of something smart to say back to *you*.

- "I never forget a face. But in your case I'll make an exception."

- "You can say whatever you want to me and I won't get mad—it's Be Kind to Animals Week."

- "I'm not upset by what you said. I know you did it without thinking . . . just like you do everything else."

- "If I agreed with you, we'd both be wrong."

- "I don't know what your problem is, but I bet it's hard to pronounce."

- "You may be trying to insult me, but I know you like me. I can see your tail wagging."

- "I really want to help you out. Which way did you come in?"

HANDY EXCUSES FOR NOT HANDING IN YOUR HOMEWORK

Here's our best advice: Do your homework. Here's our best advice if you didn't follow *that* advice: Use one of these lines.

- "I didn't do it because I didn't want to add to your workload."

- "I thought you said it was due tomorrow, and since today is *today*, I'll bring it tomorrow."

- "You'll be happy to know I told myself, 'Self, do your homework!' Unfortunately, actions speak louder than words."

- "I did my homework, but aliens took it to study how the human brain works."

- "It's true, I didn't do my homework. But since I want to impress you, I'll do it right away."

- "The truth is, I was too tired to do my homework last night. But a good night's sleep fixed all that."

- "My head told me to do it, but my hand had the final say."

- "I'm sorry I don't have my homework. My underpants were too tight, and they cut off the circulation to my brain."

CONTRACT WITH NOSY BROTHER OR SISTER RE: "STAYING OUT OF MY STUFF"

To Whom It May Concern:

I, brother/sister of _____ , do hereby state that I understand that I
   (your name)
am hereby banned from snooping in _____'s room. Furthermore,
   (your name)
I will (a) keep my paws to myself, (b) not put my nose where it does
not belong, and (c) prevent my eyeballs from "accidentally" looking
at his/her personal, private, and confidential stuff.

If I am caught breaking any of these rules, I will voluntarily hand over
my favorite toy, _____. My brother/sister will get to
   (favorite toy name)
keep this toy for at least one day while I think about my crime of
snooping and why it was oh-so-wrong.

Signed,

_____   _____
(Signature of sibling. If sibling is too young to   (Date)
sign name, marking an "X" is acceptable.)

Witnessed by:

_____   _____
(Signature of witness)   (Date)

CONTRACT WITH KID BROTHER OR SISTER RE: "HANG TIME"

To Whom It May Concern:

I, little brother/sister of _____, do hereby state that I under-
(your name)
stand the "One Time Only" rule of hanging out with _____.
(your name)
To be clear, the "One Time Only" rule means that just because an adult

has encouraged my fantastic older brother/sister to spend time with me

today, I totally get that it doesn't mean he/she will be doing so tomorrow.

Furthermore, I agree to try my hardest to be as little a pest as possible

when we're hanging out. This means I will do my best not to annoy,

embarrass, humiliate, anger, poke, prod, or sneeze on or near my

dear sibling. I will honor his/her requests not to lag behind. I will

bring him/her snacks when asked. I will keep quiet when asked. And

I will never tell anyone his/her embarrassing middle name.

Signed,

_____   _____
(Signature of sibling. If sibling is too young to   (Date)
sign name, marking an "X" is acceptable.)

Witnessed by:

_____   _____
(Signature of witness)   (Date)

About the Authors

David Borgenicht is a writer, editor, publisher, and the coauthor of all the books in the Worst-Case Scenario Survival Handbook series. He has survived dozens of childhood nightmares, including the one where you wake up naked in the middle of a test you haven't studied for. He now lives a stable adult life in Philadelphia.

As a child, **Robin Epstein** never met a worst-case scenario she didn't take on headfirst (and she has the scar on her forehead to prove it). She credits her parents for nurturing her free spirit and paying her medical bills, and she thanks them for always encouraging her to think critically and use her noggin. She lives in New York City, where her noggin comes in handy every day.

About the Illustrator

Chuck Gonzales is a New York City–based illustrator who was raised in South Dakota. His work often blends his suburban upbringing and his present urban existence. His client base has been just as diverse, including the *New York Times*, the *Washington Post*, Disney, Nickelodeon, Nick Jr., and Chronicle Books. Growing up in the Dakotas as a short, artsy, neurotic kid, he was not spared any junior high indignities.